G000135428

BEGINNING WITH SNAKES
KW-127

Contents

Photographers: American Museum of Natural History; R.W. Applegate; Dr. Herbert R. Axelrod; R. Brown; Dr. Warren Burgess; W. Deas; J. Dodd; John Dommens; Isabelle Francais; K. Freeman; M. Freiberg; Jeff Gee; Michael Gilroy; R. Hass; H. Hansen, Aquarium Berlin; R.L. Holland; B. Kahl; A. Kerstich; O. Klee; S. Kochetov; J.K. Langhammer; K. Lucas, Steinhart Aquarium; Ronald G. Markel; Dr. Sherman A. Minton; Nancy Aquarium, France; Aaron Norman; Louis Porras; P.J. Stafford; R. van Nostrand; E. Zimmermann.

Overleaf: The eastern coral snake, *Micrurus fulvius*. **Title page:** Snakes are fascinating creatures with much to offer the animal lover. They are efficient, highly evolved animals who have, unfortunately, been given a bad reputation due to misunderstanding.

© Copyright 1989 by TFH Publications Inc.

Distributed in the UNITED STATES by T.F.H. Publications, Inc., One T.F.H. Plaza, Neptune City, NJ 07753; in CANADA to the Pet Trade by H & L Pet Supplies Inc., 27 Kingston Crescent, Kitchener, Ontario N2B 2T6; Rolf C. Hagen Ltd., 3225 Sartelon Street, Montreal 382 Quebec; in CANADA to the Book Trade by Macmillan of Canada (A Division of Canada Publishing Corporation), 164 Commander Boulevard, Agincourt, Ontario M1S 3C7; in ENGLAND by T.F.H. Publications Limited, Cliveden House/Priors Way/Bray, Maidenhead, Berkshire SL6 2HP, England; in AUSTRALIA AND THE SOUTH PACIFIC by T.F.H. (Australia) Pty. Ltd., Box 149, Brookvale 2100 N.S.W., Australia; in NEW ZEALAND by Ross Haines & Son, Ltd., 18 Monmouth Street, Grey Lynn, Auckland 2, New Zealand; in SINGAPORE AND MALAYSIA by MPH Distributors (S) Pte., Ltd., 601 Sims Drive, #03/07/21, Singapore 1438; in the PHILIPPINES by Bio-Research, 5 Lippay Street, San Lorenzo Village, Makati Rizal; in SOUTH AFRICA by Multipet Pty. Ltd., 30 Turners Avenue, Durban 4001. Published by T.F.H. Publications, Inc. Manufactured in the United States of America by T.F.H. Publications, Inc.

BEGINNING WITH SNAKES

RICHARD F. STRATTON

Above: A gray rat snake, Elaphe obsoleta, emerging from its egg. In a few years it will become a solid black adult and will possibly reach six feet in length. *Right:* Snakes are sleek, dry, and cool animals that often show a surprising amount of personality. This is a European grass snake, Natrix natrix.

The World of Snakes

The purpose of this book is twofold. First, it is to demonstrate the irrationality of the fear and hatred of snakes, for both are truly nonsensical. There is no denying that venomous snakes are dangerous, but let's look at it in perspective. Even with the burgeoning human population intruding ever farther into snake habitats, there is still a very low average of deaths from snake bites. Dogs kill far more people than snakes, but dogs are not despised and feared. Furthermore, dogs may communicate diseases to humans, some of which can cause

blindness or even death. Yet the same people that are horrified to hear of a herpetologist including his sack of newly captured snakes in his sleeping bag to keep them warm would think nothing of his doing the same thing with a dog or a cat. Now I say all this as a downright maudlin dog- and cat-lover myself; however, I wanted to point out the illogic of the revulsion toward snakes.

The second purpose of the book is to recommend some specimens of non-venomous snakes for the beginning snake keeper and to provide some information on their care. The criteria for selection of species have been (1) the desirability of the snake, (2) the

ease of its maintenance, (3) how well it fares in captivity, and (4) how easily proper food is obtained for it. A further consideration has been the disposition of the animal, for even non-venomous species will bite, and while not really serious, some bites are not easily laughed off, either! Still, it is amazing how even ornery snakes will become tame when handled regularly. Until you develop a certain "snake sense," it would probably be best to handle such ornery individuals while wearing heavy gloves and—if it is a large specimen several feet long—a heavy jacket, too.

The reader will note that venomous snakes have been left

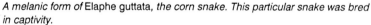

A melanic form of Elaphe guttata, *the corn snake. This particular snake was bred in captivity.*

A common garter snake, Thamnophis sirtalis sirtalis, *caught in the act of eating a frog.*

out of the chapter describing the various recommended species. Obviously they are not for beginners; even professional herpetologists have been bitten and have died. Anyway, why keep them? Only a small fraction of snakes are poisonous. Unless you are going into the study of hemotoxins and neurotoxins, you'll find the poisonous species generally less interesting. If non-poisonous snakes are too tame for you, just remember that non-venomous snakes kill and eat venomous ones—and that they also include an occasional mongoose in their diet!

It is a gift to be able to see beauty and wonder where others find only ugliness and fear. But it is not a blessing bestowed by the gods, for the trait can be learned—and very quickly, too! In a matter of days—even hours—I have seen students in my science class turn around 180 degrees in their attitudes toward snakes. And I have been amused to see comely young student teachers, at first paralyzed by fear and loathing, later proudly displaying in their hands one of our old friends (the classroom snakes) to their husbands (who usually did their manly best not to betray their own fear!).

Although it is difficult for me not to be scornful of the hatred so many hold for snakes, it is not beyond my understanding. I, too, was once fearful of them, and, of

The European viper, Vipera berus, a common species which is responsible for many cases of snakebite each year. Vipers are never recommended for keeping in captivity, as all species are venomous to some degree.

course, for that reason I hated them. "Watch out for snakes!" was the admonition my sister and I received each time we left the small mountain cabin in which we spent our earliest years. It was true that rattlesnakes abounded in the area, but we never saw even one—except in our dreams! For many years both of us had the same nightmare, being admonished to beware of snakes, only to look outside and find there was no place to step, so crowded was the ground with the writhing creatures!

The revulsion toward snakes was to be deeply imbedded in my fibers for years to come. When I attended college, I worked part-time as a night watchman on campus. Finding the door to one of the rooms in the museum building unlocked one night, I warily inspected the darkness within, half expecting an intruder to still be there. The beam from my light fell upon a gigantic jar filled with preserved snakes of all sizes and colors. The shock could not have been greater if I had looked upon Medusa herself.

It is amusing now to think back on that incident, for now I regard snakes as marvelous creatures— magnificent little predators highly evolved and awesomely adapted to exploit their particular niche in nature. And, believe it or not, they do have personalities and are

An Eastern hognose snake, Heterodon platyrhinos. *Snakes are individuals, just as people are, and each particular creature has a unique personality.*

Close-up of the head of Chondropython viridis, *the green tree python. This species is similar to the emerald tree boa.*

remarkably individualistic. That doesn't mean they are intelligent, of course, for part of their "personality" consists of some of the dumb things they do! However, they are as intelligent as other reptiles, although, admittedly, that is not exactly high praise!

Consider our classroom snakes. Although "Stella" (being one of mine) is one of my favorite snakes, perhaps we should start first with "Arnold," a handsome little gopher snake belonging to my good friend and fellow science teacher, Jim Johnson. (Incidentally, the reader will note

Tree snakes, like this snake of the genus Elaphe, are often bright green in color, and they sometimes have elongated heads. Keep in mind that some species of tree snakes are venomous.

that all of our snakes have names. Among the reasons for this is that innocuous names tend to break down the satanic image of the poor maligned serpents in question.) Arnold has been in Jim's class for fourteen years (I told you snakes were of very low intelligence—Arnold hasn't passed that course yet!), and he has been a constant source of delight to countless students. Never once has he bitten anyone; in fact, he seems to enjoy being handled. So trustworthy has Arnold been that he has been unofficially dubbed as "Old Saint Snake," and the only worry about leaving him unsupervised with the students is what they might do to him!

On the other hand, once a month Arnold demonstrates just what a dangerous animal he can be—to a rat! So renowned is Arnold's reputation as a rodent killer par excellence that tickets could be sold to witness his monthly feedings. The rat never knows what hit it, so quick and clean is Arnold's kill. Immediately sensing a rodent in his cage, Arnold runs it down, striking quicker than the eye can follow and rapidly coiling around the rat, snuffing out its life by restriction of respiratory and cardiac functions. Then the students watch entranced as the little snake locates the head and proceeds with the seemingly impossible task of engulfing his gigantic "meal." Thus, Arnold demonstrates what

efficient predators snakes are, but who knows how many former students—most of them now adults—would have been the all-too-typical snake haters if they had not been privileged to have known Arnold?

Then there is Ringo, my baby kingsnake. If any group of snakes has enjoyed relative immunity to the general hatred of the public, it is the kingsnakes. And for what reason? Simply because most people are aware that kingsnakes will kill and eat rattlesnakes. Of course, among ophiophiles (snake lovers) this trait is of dubious distinction—especially since kingsnakes will also eat other snakes. Since nearly all snake keepers are concerned with conservation of snake species, they are loath to utilize any specimens as food. Consequently, most of us are ambivalent about keeping kingsnakes. On the one hand, they are among the finest of snakes, generally quite handsome and usually docile with humans (once adapted to captivity). On the other, they often must be fed snakes or lizards. Since we also keep lizards in our science room, we have a partial solution in that we can feed the lizards that are not doing well in captivity. The amazing thing about Ringo (as with all baby kingsnakes) is the size of the lizards he is able to kill (by constriction) and engulf. As innocuous as Ringo appears, he is the snake we must watch most

A boa constrictor writhing its way through the grass. Boa constrictors possess an automatic reflex that causes them to clamp down on any movement.

closely—or else keep him in his own cage—for he views all other snakes as potential meals!

Then there are Oscar and Mayer, two garter snakes kept together in the same cage by a third science teacher, Larry Wing. These two little snakes put on an absolutely absurd display during feeding. Two goldfish are dropped into their water bowl, and bedlam erupts! Oscar and Mayer each want the other's fish. First, a frantic "apple bobbing" orgy ensues. Then after each one finally secures a fish, they both

The California mountain kingsnake, Lampropeltis zonata, *is a beautiful species, but, unfortunately, it is difficult to obtain.*

scurry around the cage, each holding his head high with his prize dangling from his mouth and each intent on preventing the other from taking his fish, while hurriedly trying to wolf it down so that he can go after the other guy's! In spite of all this shameless competition for food, Oscar and Mayer never fight, and between feedings (several days) the two snakes are as likely as not huddled together. Discounting predation (which, contrary to public opinion, is not fighting), snakes rarely, if ever, seem inclined to fight. Some tropical species are reported to hold territories during mating seasons and fight off other males, but this is rare among snakes—the exception rather than the rule.

My own little garter snake, Gertrude, lives by herself and spends most of her time huddled in her cardboard "duplex." Each morning she dangles her head over the water bowl to see if I will

A strikingly colored milk snake, Lampropeltis triangulum. *Milk snakes are very desirable as pets, but they are strictly regulated by wildlife protection laws.*

A gray rat snake, Elaphe obsoleta quadrivittata, *resting in a tree.*

feed her. Snakes are like humans (alas!) in that they like to eat more food than is good for them. So Gertrude gets fed no more often than one fish every other day. On occasion she can fast for a week, then eat two or three fish at one feeding. She will take fish from my fingers, but I usually feed her in her water bowl. Any time that I take the top off her cage, she rushes to the water bowl to see if I will feed her. You can almost see the disappointment on her face if she doesn't get fed, and she finally withdraws unhappily back to her duplex. As she glides into her quarters, I am left to ponder my strength of will in regard to her diet and what is good for her and how

weak is that same will when it comes to my own diet!

Finally, we come to Stella, my boa constrictor. Beautiful creature that she is, I named her after my mother-in-law (who has since threatened to kill me for that "honor"!). Presently over six feet in length, Stella is of particular interest to students, and she is another "Saint Snake" candidate, having not once bitten a student— even when they have unintentionally hurt her. She likes to "climb" around their bodies. To prevent any panicking among the students, I warn them that she is surprisingly strong and an automatic reflex will cause her to "clamp down" on any movement

Microcephalophis gracilis, *a small-headed sea snake. All sea snakes are venomous, and many never leave the sea, not even to breed or give birth.*

on their part. Thus, if she is wrapped around an arm and the arm is flexed or moved, she will tighten her coils. The same is true if she is wrapped around a neck! But there is no danger, for with cessation of movement she relaxes her grip. She spends most of her time asleep on her perch (a shelf at the top of her large cage). But on the infrequent occasions that she does move, for example down to the bottom of the cage to get a drink, she commands attention with her natural grace and beauty.

Knowing a snake personally nearly always dispels negative feelings toward at least that species, if not snakes in general. However, it would be a mistake to think that experience with one individual specimen qualifies one as an authority on a species, for snakes are quite individualistic, a fact aptly demonstrated by "Dillinger." Although he looks like Arnold's twin brother and is of the same species, Dillinger is the Mr. Hyde counterpart to Arnold's Dr. Jekyll! He refuses to be handled and flattens his head, hisses, vibrates his tail, and strikes viciously at any that disturb him. Generally speaking, though, gopher snakes do become tame. Later on in the book, as we discuss species, we will be talking about the average disposition; always remember that there are exceptions and that snakes are quite variable.

Below: A northern rosy boa, Lichanura trivirgata roseofusca. ***Opposite:*** *A striking corn snake,* Elaphe guttata.

Above: A slender, rapid-moving whipsnake, Masticophis, *a harmless snake from the deserts of the western United States.* **Right:** A very stout, slow-moving viper, Vipera berus, *a venomous snake of Eurasian woods and marshes.*

The Nature of the Beast

While I am often dismayed at the hatred that is generally directed at snakes, it is difficult not to be equally scornful of those that "feel sorry" for snakes because of their lack of limbs. Save your sentiments, my friends, for the snake is successful primarily because he does not have limbs! He is able to get into places (and out of them) precisely because he does not have cumbersome legs or arms and also because of his shape. In fact, the snake evolved from ancestors that had limbs; that is, the lizards. Indeed, some lizards are legless and resemble snakes; their eyelids and external ears give them away, though. Snakes have a fixed transparent eyelid (the brille) that gives them their fixed stare. All snakes are

predators (although some prey only on insects and worms), and all swallow their prey whole. A measure of the snake's success as a predator is the fact that, for its size, it is able to eat the largest prey of any vertebrate. How often a snake feeds depends on the size of the snake vis-a-vis the size of its prey.

SNAKE SENSES

Sight: Since the snake has a transparent eyelid, the lens itself is colored, apparently to help filter out strong light. The lens is a fixed spherical shape, and focusing is accomplished by muscles that move the lens itself in relation to the retina. Although an ingenious system, it limits the animal's versatility in regard to focusing, so snakes are generally quite nearsighted. They do detect motion quite well, and most have a wide field of vision. They have some cones in the retina and presumably can see color.

Nerodia sipedon comprenicauda. *Snakes have rather weak eyesight and are rather sensitive to light.*

A common garter snake, Thamnophis sirtalis sirtalis. *Snakes are very sensitive to ground vibrations rather than to airborne sounds.*

Hearing: The snakes have no outer ear. Instead, the bones that connect the inner ear to the outer in the amphibians and in reptiles other than snakes are in the snakes connected to the lower jaw. Apparently it is more important for snakes to "hear" ground vibrations (footsteps, etc.) than airborne sounds. So snakes, while not exactly deaf, do not hear what we hear. On the other hand, they hear what we cannot. They would make great earthquake predictors—if only we could train them to signal us in some way when one is imminent!

Smell: As nearly everyone knows, a snake smells with its tongue. The reason a snake's tongue is forked is so that it will fit into two pockets in the mouth that form part of the taste-smell organ known as Jacobson's organ. The flickering two-pronged tongue picks up molecules from the outside. When the tongue is retracted, its tips are inserted into the pits of the sensitive organ. If we observe a snake closely, however, we will note that it also has nostrils, and it turns out that these function quite well. However, the tongue provides a super sense of "taste-smell"! It is actively used when a snake is hungry or checking out its surroundings. A good analogy would be to compare our sense of smell with that of a trail hound,

Above: The diamond python, Morelia spilotes, *is a large species found over most of Australia and New Guinea. There are depressions on some of the lip scales that serve as heat detectors, much like those of pit vipers.* **Opposite:** The green mamba, Dendroapsis angusticeps, *is one of the most feared venomous snakes. The slender head and body of this tree-dwelling snake prove false the old adage that poisonous snakes can be recognized by their arrow-shaped head.*

such as a Redbone Hound. Thus, a snake's nostrils would be like our own sense of smell and the tongue would compare to that of the Redbone. As a matter of fact, a snake will trail prey or even a potential mate with use of the super scenting powers that his tongue provides him.

Heat detectors: Many snakes—especially those that hunt warmblooded prey by night—have special organs that detect the heat given off by endothermic (warmblooded) animals. The pit vipers (which include the rattlesnakes) are so called because of such an organ that is located in a pit that resides between the eye and nostril on each side of the head. Other snakes have heat sensors, too, such as some of the members of the family Boidae (pythons, boas, and anacondas), but they are located on the lips and the jaws.

Touch and pain: Although snakes have no larynx and therefore cannot cry out, they do feel pain quite acutely. The only way that they can respond is by trying to get away or by biting. So sensitive are some rat snakes (and others) that if bitten by a rat or mouse while feeding, they sometimes will henceforth forego such fare (which can create a problem, since they usually won't eat anything else!). Most respond in some way to the slightest touch on almost any part of the body.

ANATOMY

Two features of the snake are especially distinctive: its elongate shape and the fact that it often engulfs extremely large prey. Special structures have been called into play to accommodate the latter fact. For one thing, the trachea extends out along the floor of the mouth and has incomplete cartilaginous rings. The glottis openings are near the front of the lower jaw. Such structures allow the animal to breathe during nearly all the time that it is engulfing its meal. In addition, loose stretchable ligaments allow the jaw to distend and accommodate extremely large bodies.

A further aid to engulfing large prey is the elongate stomach, which is possible precisely because of the shape of the snake. In fact, the alimentary canal is accommodated extremely well by the snake's shape, without a lot of needless twisting around back and forth, at least not anywhere near to the degree that it is in other animals such as ourselves. With the paired organs there is a problem, though, because there simply is not the width for "normal" placement of these structures. The snake's solution has been to either "stack" the pair one above the other or eliminate one of them. For example, the more advanced snakes have only one lung.

Skin: For protection snakes are

A milk snake, Lampropeltis triangulum, *which is lacking the usual yellow coloration. Some herpetologists assign this variety to* Lampropeltis triangulum hondurensis.

scaly, but theirs are not the individual scales as is the case with the fishes. That is, they are all interconnected by soft folds of skin which provide flexibility. Consequently, as the scales wear out they cannot be replaced one at a time. For that reason, snakes shed their entire skins at more-or-less regular intervals. This is another way that snakes are qualitatively different from us, for humans continually produce keratin from the inside as the old material is worn away from the outside. With snakes a complete new skin is grown underneath the old one, and after it is fully formed the animal sheds or molts its old skin. To accomplish this, the

Above: *A reticulated python,* Python reticulatis, *makes a satisfactory pet, but its food requirements (small live or frozen mammals such as baby mice) are rather difficult for beginners to fulfill.* **Below:** *A gopher snake,* Pituophis melanoleucus.

Above: The eastern timber rattlesnake, Crotalus horridus, *is still found in parts of the eastern United States, but is becoming more and more scarce.* **Below:** *The scarlet snake,* Cemophora coccinea, *is similar to the various species of coral king-snakes and milk snakes; it has, however, an unmarked belly and fewer blotches.*

snake secretes a fluid between the old and new skins. This gives the eyes a cloudy appearance. A few days after the cloudiness appears, the snake sheds his skin from head to tail, often in one piece. Most species look their best right after they have shed. As the skin gets older, the colors don't show through as well.

REPRODUCTION

Most snakes lay eggs with a tough leathery shell and an elongate shape. Some, however, bear living young. In either case, with rare exceptions, the snake then pays no attention to the eggs or young; in fact, it may eat its own progeny. The same is true of most fishes, amphibians, and the other reptiles, too.

Whether the snake is egglaying or livebearing, internal fertilization is necessary. It became so with the advent of the amniote egg in the earliest reptiles. It may be hard to picture amorous snakes, but it usually goes something like this. When ready to mate, the female serpent gives off a scent, even leaving a scent trail. The first lucky male that crosses the scent follows the trail with a flickering tongue until he finds the female. There are various ways, depending upon the species, that the male stimulates the female to present her cloaca. Whatever the method, the female nearly always considers the male a suave lover. Male snakes have two intromittent organs, each called a hemipene. Much to the female's relief, the male only uses one organ at a time. In fact, it may be that a particular male favors, or only uses at all, one of his hemipenes.

Mating may last several hours. In fact, the hemipene of the male snake is often furnished with spines and hooks that serve as a locking mechanism to ensure successful fertilization. The snakes lie mostly motionless during this time, and the male may often grip the female with his mouth. Usually the female is completely passive, but in some species an elaborate courtship dance takes place before mating. When the female lays the eggs, she normally goes off with nary a backward glance. Instinct, however, will usually dictate that she select a suitable (in regard to humidity, temperature, and safety) spot for them. Some species do provide some parental care. Some of the elapids (cobras) build a nest and both parents defend it. Some of the pythons also stay with the eggs, and recent research indicates that the female is able to elevate her body temperature somehow (probably by tensing various muscles) for incubation purposes.

UNIQUE TRAITS

While the snake's lack of limbs and his peculiar structures impose certain limitations, they also provide unique advantages that

A common garter snake. A snake's first line of defense is to try to escape from an enemy. Its elongated body allows it access to many unusual hiding places.

have enabled him to become one of the most successful of reptiles. The sea snakes, for example, are the only reptiles to adapt completely to life in the sea. (Sea turtles return to land to lay eggs.) The snake's body is able to climb trees, move fairly rapidly in a variety of ways across different types of terrain, and all snakes seem to be at least fair swimmers. (When I speak of moving "fairly rapidly" across terrain, I am speaking in comparison to other reptiles. A normal man can outrun all snakes—including the racers.) A few species can even fly—well, actually, they glide, but still, isn't even that impressive?

Now for a word on the snake's protective mechanisms and a look at the dark side of a snake's nature which may have influenced mankind to brand the snake a villainous and evil creature. A snake's usual defense is to simply try to get away. There are not many animals he can outrun, but he can go places they cannot— into a rock pile, under logs, down holes, etc. But if trapped, he may put on a threatening display. He will flatten his head, vibrate his tail, hiss loudly, and strike viciously. Some species are all bluff and will strike with the mouth closed and absolutely will not bite. Others, however, will bite, but other than possibly causing a secondary infection—and

A Burmese python, Python molurus bivittatus, *requires very large living quarters. In addition, Burmese Pythons must be licensed in some areas. A snake this size should never be left alone near children.*

Even desert snakes such as this striped whipsnake, Masticophis lateralis, *cannot survive more than brief exposure to direct midday sunlight unless they have cool, shaded retreats available.*

hurting!—the bites are of little consequence. Finally, if seized, many snakes have a musk gland that allows them to emit a foul-smelling odor. In addition, some species evert the cloaca and wrap around their tormentor, smearing him with fecal matter. Disgusting? Perhaps, but undeniably an ingenious protective mechanism. Who knows how many coyotes and other animals have seized a snake for a snack and then, after some of the foregoing treatment, suddenly lost their appetite?

Temperature control: Another feature of snakes that some humans find repulsive is that snakes are "coldblooded." Technically, this is called ectothermy (as opposed to the endothermy of warmblooded animals, such as birds and mammals, that produce and control their body temperature internally). In other words, the snake's heat source is external, and he tends to be the same temperature as his environment. However, most snakes have a fairly narrow temperature range in which their bodies function well. Consequently, they do attempt to control their body temperature, seeking the warmth of the sun (or rocks) when cold and seeking shade and moisture when hot.

The nature of snakes is diverse, and generalizations are often risky. So complex are the various adaptations that a chapter like this can be but a mere primer on the marvelous adaptations and characteristics of snakes. Hopefully the reader's interest will be piqued enough to motivate further study.

Care and Feeding of Serpents

One of the main problems in keeping snakes is in getting them to eat. I have circumvented this problem somewhat by recommending snakes that feed well in captivity. However, a primary reason for failure to eat is that the snake is in a constant state of fear in the quarters you provided. Luckily, the remedy is simple. All you need is a good hiding place for your snake, as snakes are by nature hiders. When provided with a "home" into which he can retire at will, a miraculous change comes over the snake. He feels more secure and will venture forth for food and water. Wooden or cardboard "huts" make excellent hiding places, although purist-minded snake keepers like a natural-looking cage (or terrarium) and might prefer bark or a pile of rocks for the hiding place. Still, the snake is perfectly satisfied with a hut, and he is far more accessible to his keeper in this way.

DIETARY NEEDS

In any case, the easy species to keep are the ones that eat rodents or fish, as "feeder" goldfish are available at many pet stores on a year-round basis. A word may be in order here about rodents, specifically rats. First, strangely enough, rats or even mice can be a danger to snakes. If the snake doesn't eat the rodents, they may chew on the snake and damage him badly. The poor serpent's only

defense is to either get away (which he cannot do in a cage) or kill the rodents (which he won't do if he isn't hungry). For that reason, many people kill the rodents before feeding them to the snake. They tap the mouse or rat on the head with a little hammer or stick, then move it in front of the snake's head until he grabs it. (Most snake keepers will want to use forceps to allow for a margin of error on the snake's part!) The snake, if it is a constrictor, will go ahead and "kill" his prey—even though it is already dead. Feeding in this way, there is no danger of any damage to the snake. Here again, though, there is some divergence of opinion on how things should be done. Since snakes have a tendency to become lazy in captivity, some snake keepers prefer to do whatever is needed to counteract this trend. Some prefer to have the snake make its own kill. They put only one rodent in at a time and remove it if the snake isn't hungry. If the snake is a klutz and grabs the rodent in the wrong place or throws the coils in an awkward, ineffective manner that allows the rodent to gnaw on the snake, then the snake keeper goes into action and taps the rodent unconscious (for the rodent's sake as well, for this would not be a quick and clean kill by the snake).

A further word may be in order here about the rodents. Doubtless many kind-hearted persons would

Oxyrhopus rhombifer, one of the 2500 species of colubrid snakes.

Above: *Vipera ursini, a fairly common viper found in southern Europe.* ***Opposite:*** *A handful of gray-banded kingsnakes,* Lampropeltis alternata mexicana. *Fortunately, it is now possible to breed some of the popular snakes in captivity and thus relieve the strain placed on natural populations by collecting.*

be horrified to see a snake constrict and eat a rat or a mouse. Some might even be moved to contact humane-oriented groups. While such sensitivity is understandable, it is not logical, for it fails to take into account the millions of wild rats that are subject to constant predation—not to mention the trapping and poisoning carried out by man! The rats that die at the "hands" of our snakes are but a small fraction of the rats that die every day, and their deaths are generally easier than those of their brethren in the wilds.

Now, having said all of that, let me interject one more thing about the rodents. First of all, while it is difficult at first to feed these animals to snakes, it gets easier after a while as a sort of calloused attitude develops. To counter this

A variety of boa constrictor, Boa constrictor occidentalis. *Snakes are escape artists; therefore, you must make sure their quarters are very secure.*

An albino form of the California mountain kingsnake, Lampropeltis getulus californiae. *This snake is a banded phase of the subspecies.*

trend, we need to remind ourselves that a rat is a marvelous animal that is probably the most intelligent of all the rodents. A bunny may look cuter and evoke more sympathy, but a rat is smarter and much more like a human. In fact, in my college psychology courses we worked with rats under the premise that "Man is a bigger, better rat." To which some added, "Well, bigger, anyway!"

While it is true that rats compete with us for food and get into our garbage and grain—and, yes, even carry diseases—they have been of tremendous benefit to mankind, too. We are all aware of the cancer studies being done on

Opposite: This large boa constrictor could easily be more than this little girl could handle without parental assistance. It is never wise to allow your constrictor to coil around your neck, even if it is relatively tame.

rats. (One cartoon character, asked what was the leading cause of cancer, answered "Mouse abuse!") There has also been tremendous medical research in other areas. Rats are of a small size, are conveniently kept, and are usually easy to handle. They have been heavily involved in the testing and development of many new medical compounds. They have helped make the study of nutrition a science. And research with rats has given us insights into the nature of learning and general psychology.

Now don't starve your snakes because of the foregoing diatribe, but try to keep in mind the needs of the rodents (if you grow your own) and do your best to prevent or alleviate any suffering on their part.

ACCOMMODATIONS

Having the snake escape is unnerving and can nip the snake keeper's career in the bud, so an escape-proof snake cage is a necessity. It must be kept in mind that it is a snake's business to be able to get into and out of difficult places, and for that reason he is by nature an escape artist. On the other hand, the cage should have ventilation. However, there should be very little screening on the side of the cage, as the snake will get abrasions on his snout that are susceptible to infection. For small snakes, an aquarium is an acceptable cage. Wooden cages

with glass fronts can be constructed fairly easily for larger specimens.

A water bowl should be provided for your snake, and it should have a flat base to prevent overturning. It is essential that the cage be kept dry, as snakes can get skin blisters from too damp an environment. On the other hand, the snake should not become dehydrated, either. Hence the water bowl, which should be replaced with fresh water at least two or three times a week. Since snakes may like to soak their bodies occasionally, it is desirable to have a water bowl large enough to allow the snake to crawl in—just be sure it is not so deep the snake can't get out again.

Most snakes should be fed once every two or three weeks. While a snake that feeds well is a boon and solace to the snake keeper, it is amazing how long a snake can go without food. As an example, Pat Cooney, a very knowledgeable snake keeper, once had a sand boa get out of a bag in his car in the late summer. Pat was certain the snake had been stolen by someone, as he was sure the bag had been tied securely. Late the following spring, Pat was out collecting rattlesnakes with his wife for a researcher who was doing hemotoxin studies. By the end of the evening, they had several rattlesnakes in a bag in the rear seat of the car and were headed for home. As he was driving along, Pat's hair fairly stood on end as he was suddenly aware of a snake crawling across his ankle. Naturally, he thought only in terms of one of the rattlesnakes having escaped from the bag. After an extremely cautious roadside stop and glacierlike movements to obtain light, the long-lost sand boa was illuminated! Other than being a little desiccated, the snake appeared none the worse for wear.

Since a dry and clean cage is very important for a snake's well-being, the selection of a suitable substrate is essential. Here again, there is some difference of opinion. Certainly, for relative novices the substrate should be either sand or paper toweling. (Newspapers would probably be all right, too, although there is some worry about possible toxicity of the ink.) Every two or three months, the sand (if that is what you opted for) should be taken out and washed with water in a bucket, preferably without soap. Just run the water through the sand while stirring it until the water runs clear. Now you can either wait six months for the sand to dry or put it in pans in the oven and bake it dry. Remember, dryness is important! If you're using paper toweling, simply replace it as it becomes dirty. One important ally in keeping the snake cage dry is the fact that snakes do not produce liquid urine; urine is instead excreted in crystals that usually appear as a chalky white solid substance.

DISEASE

If you keep snakes long enough, you eventually will have snakes that have mites or mouth rot—the two main curses of a snake keeper's life! Luckily, both of these afflictions are relatively easily treated. Mouth rot is actually an inflammation (caused by infection) of the tissues of the mouth. The gums become tender, sometimes the snake can't close his mouth properly, and he will eventually refuse to eat. Some have treated the infection successfully with antiseptic mouthwashes applied with a cotton applicator. However, a solution of sulfamethiazine applied in the same way is more often the recommended treatment.

For control of mites, prevention can involve suspending a couple of inches of a no-pest insecticide strip in the cage. The more cautious snake keepers suspend the strip outside the cage, near the ventilation ports, and that would be my recommendation, for it must be remembered that snakes are very vulnerable to toxic compounds. A non-toxic powder, available at your pet shop, can be used once the snake is infested. The powder can be sprinkled on the snake and in the cage and left for a few days. Then clean out the cage completely and

A corn snake, Elaphe guttata. *Every snake's cage should be provided with a water bowl, and its water should be fresh and cool at all times.*

wash it down with clean water. (Incidentally, if you use this powder, get it in its pure form, making sure that no insecticides have been mixed with it.) Some snake keepers prefer to drown the mites by bathing the snake, but this requires time and much personal attention.

Many snakes can be kept at room temperature—none should be exposed to anywhere near freezing temperatures!—but tropical species will need a source of warmth. This can be provided by a light fixture, preferably with a rheostat switch in order to vary the intensity and heat of the light. A thermostatically controlled source of heat is ideal but not absolutely necessary.

Finally, although experience is the best teacher, you can learn a lot from fellow (and more

Above: Pythons often lay fertile eggs in captivity, and it is not uncommon for these to be successfully incubated if proper management is provided. These ball pythons, Python regius, are hatching after incubation. **Opposite:** The successful snake keeper will provide clean, roomy cages for all of his charges.

experienced) ophiophiles, too, so it might behoove you to get to know a few. Check the advertisements in your local paper for anyone selling snakes. Best of all, ask your pet dealer about any "herp" clubs. These are a great place to learn about snakes and to do a little swapping or even bargain buying. These groups usually provide some sort of program at their meetings and even have picnics and parties. You'll have a good time getting together with these people and occasionally celebrate by burning a mongoose in effigy!

Below: A pair of gray-banded kingsnake hatchlings, Lampropeltis alternata mexicana. *Opposite:* A rainbow boa, Epicrates cenchria.

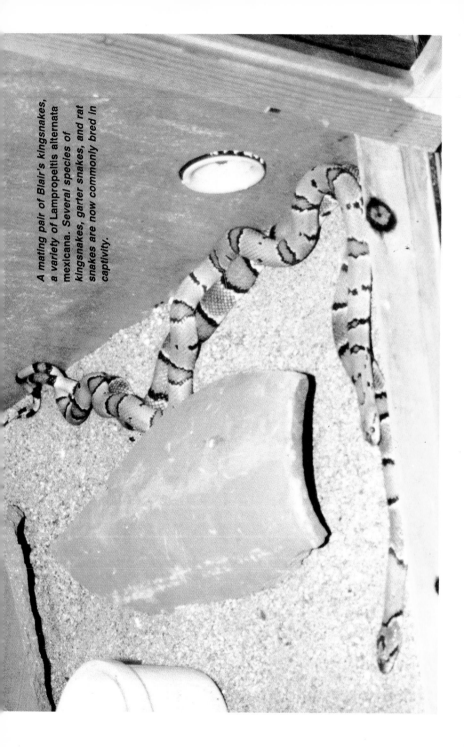

A mating pair of Blair's kingsnakes, a variety of Lampropeltis alternata mexicana. Several species of kingsnakes, garter snakes, and rat snakes are now commonly bred in captivity.

Above: This well-designed snake room includes an artificial incubator for snake eggs. *Below:* The gray-banded kingsnake, Lampropeltis alternata mexicana, *is a beautiful species that is popular with advanced hobbyists.*

Recommended Species

First, when we start talking about individual snake species, we need to start being at least a little cognizant of scientific names. The problem with popular names is that they vary from one region to another. Take, for example, our old friend Arnold, which we called a gopher snake. That is, in some places he is a gopher snake, while in others he would be a pine snake. In other regions he would be called a bull snake. However, Arnold also has a scientific name, *Pituophis melanoleucus*, and that name stays the same regardless of where we take him or find him in the whole world! Scientific names are useful, too, in knowing relationships. For example, any time we see the generic name *Lampropeltis* (which means "shiny skin"), we know we have some sort of kingsnake—even if it is called a "milk snake" or a "king coral." Further, it might be useful to know what the families of snakes are, even though the snakes we talk about will belong to only two of the families. Here are the ten snake families.

Typhlopidae (blind snakes), 200 species, non-venomous.

Leptotyphlopidae (thread snakes), 40 species, non-venomous.

Anilidae (pipe snakes), ten species, non-venomous.

Boidae (pythons and boas), 100 species, non-venomous.

Uropeltidae (shieldtails), 40 species, non-venomous.

Xenopeltidae (sunbeam snake), one species, non-venomous.

Colubridae (colubrids or common snakes), 2500 species, non-venomous (except for rear-fanged species).

Elapidae (cobras), 150 species, venomous.

Hydrophidae (sea snakes), 50 species, venomous.

Viperidae (vipers), 80 species, venomous.

Perhaps it should be pointed out that work on classification is going on all the time, and some herpetologists would list the families differently, but the foregoing table is generally accepted. In any case, taxonomists working in a particular area of specialization are bound to break it down into a number of subfamilies and perhaps erect a system of superfamilies, too. For many years now, however, biologists have pretty much worked around the ten-family concept that is listed here.

Generally speaking, I am only listing species that will do well in captivity and that are low-maintenance species. One of the charms of snake keeping is that snakes do not require constant

Opposite: A strikingly colored corn snake, Elaphe guttata. *Corn snakes are good climbers and enjoy trees in their cages.*

attention, and it is possible to go off on a two-week vacation without terrifying your neighbors by recruiting them to care for your snakes. To reiterate, an important point in snake keeping is the diet of the snake and the availability of its food supply. Snakes that will take a variety of food are a real pleasure. Unfortunately, some of the most beautiful and desirable snakes are very specialized feeders that will accept little variation in their diet. It is often possible, however, to fool these specimens into eating the "wrong" food, since snakes are so dependent upon smell in their recognition of food. Thus a kingsnake may be induced to eat a rodent that has been kept where snakes have been or that has been rubbed so that it smells like a snake.

One of the reasons why many snake keepers are so concerned that their charges not become lazy snakes is because they want their animals to be at their best. A more important motive is that they would like to have their snakes reproduce in captivity. Most snake keepers are naturalists and, as such, are concerned about diminishing snake populations. In fact, some even feel guilty about buying snakes because they do not want to encourage snake collecting—especially of endangered species. A partial balm for the conscience is to attempt to breed snakes and release the progeny into the wild. But release them where? The primary reason for the diminishment of snake populations is habitat destruction.

Besides having no place to release the snakes, there are other reasons that militate against breeding serpents for the purpose of releasing them into the wild. Biologists would be concerned about the introduction of diseases into the wild fauna. There would also be concern about possible alterations of the wild genetic pool and worries, too, about imposing too much competition for food among the wild inhabitants. The main purpose behind breeding snakes should be to sell them among snake-keeping hobbyists, thus relieving the pressure of collection upon the wild populations.

Many nations have laws protecting wild snakes from unauthorized collectors. For this reason, the best way to go about obtaining a pet snake is to contact a pet shop. Many species are readily available; if the snake that interests you is not, your pet shop dealer can help you locate another source.

FAMILY BOIDAE

The boids are among the most popular snakes for the snake keeper—with good reason. They are generally big snakes, are handsomely marked, and are of a spectacular appearance. The

The African spitting cobra or ringhals, Hemachatus haemachates, *is able to spit its venom forward under pressure so that it travels several feet. This snake usually aims at reflective surfaces such as the eyes. Whether one is hit by a spray of venom or receives a bite from any cobra, the danger is the same—very serious.*

reader should be aware that this family is generally broken up into two subfamilies: Boinae and Pythoninae. Generally speaking, the pythons are Old World snakes that lay eggs, while the boas are New World snakes that give birth to living young. There are other differences, such as the bones in the skull, but these are mainly of interest to the taxonomist. The pythons are the most widely distributed. Although not all boids are large, these are generally known as the giant snakes. The honor for the largest snake in the world can be split between the anaconda (a boa), which is generally the heaviest of snakes, and the reticulated python, which

A boa constrictor, Boa constrictor constrictor. *Boids are known as giant snakes since so many of them reach a very large size.*

A Fiji boa, Candoia, *which is wrapped around itself.*

is the longest. The boas are confined to the New World, with the exception of two genera in Malagasy and one in the South Pacific. The giants of the group are confined to the tropics, probably because of the difficulty of heating and cooling such large bodies in less stable temperature regions. The boids are relatively primitive snakes. They have two lungs, a hip girdle (but it is not attached to the spine), and vestigial pelvic bones that are remnants of what were once hindlegs. These remnants protrude as "spurs" and are more prominent in the male. In fact, the spurs may be completely absent in females.

Boa Constrictor (*Boa constrictor*)

This species is one of the most popularly kept of all snake species, and it has much to

Boa constrictors vary considerably in both coloration and personality.

Natrix maura. *Snakes of the genus* Natrix *are colorful but are usually bad-tempered.*

commend it. Attractively marked, the species attains a length of about 11 or 12 feet. The disposition and coloration of the snake vary somewhat with the origin of the animals. The ones from Colombia are generally the most desirable on both counts. The body of such a specimen has a rosy flush when mature. One of the most important secrets to keeping one of these individuals in good shape is in maintaining the temperature between 75 and 85 degrees. With tropical species such as this, it is probably worth purchasing a thermostatically controlled source of heat.

While young and small specimens are more delicate, half of the fun with this species is obtaining a little guy and watching him grow. Young specimens may be fed "pinkies" (baby mice) or, better yet, half-grown mice, and later on they will take baby chicks. In about five years, your boa constrictor will be about six or seven feet long and will be easily taking large adult rats. You can distinguish the sexes at this time by the spurs which are more prominent in the male. This species is a good candidate for reproduction. Simply keep a pair together and try to provide hiding places for the young. Remove them (or the parents) once they appear.

Emerald Tree Boa (*Corallus caninus*)

This is one of the most desirable of snakes—in terms of appearance, that is! Unfortunately, it doesn't take to handling well, and it has the dentition to inflict a serious bite. The best way to tame this species is to begin with a heavy jacket and heavy gloves. Pick it up, giving it plenty of support, and try to make like a tree as much as possible. The snake will very likely settle down, but be careful about people passing by you, as the animal may be tempted to strike by their motion.

Youngsters of this species are pink to orange, turning greenish as they mature. Found in South America, tree boas spend most of their time in trees, coiled in such a way as to resemble a bunch of bananas or other similar fruit. They feed on birds, squirrels, and lizards. For some reason, they do not always eat well in captivity. They will, however, usually take chicks or small rodents.

Rosy Boa (*Lichanura trivirgata*)

Although the rosy boa is small, it is slow-moving and is nearly as sluggish as its giant tropical cousins. Most people rave about these snakes because they rarely—almost never—bite. However, they are not always good feeders in captivity, although they will usually take mice. They are one of two boa species found in the United States, the other being the rubber boa (*Charina bottae*), which is sometimes called the two-headed boa because it has a thick, rounded tail resembling a second head. Both species average about two feet in length.

Cuban Boa (*Epicrates angulifer*)

This boa reaches about ten feet maximum size. It feeds primarily on bats, and, like the tree boa, it spends quite a bit of time in trees. (All boids should have a branch to climb on in their cage and also a perch.) This is one of those species with labial pits that function as heat sensors. In captivity, the Cuban boa will accept rodents—which is nice, because bat-gathering is no fun at all! This is a species that can be aggressive, so it may be time to get out those heavy gloves and jacket again. However, to be completely honest, I am a little reluctant to characterize a species as aggressive or docile, not just because of individual variation within a species but also because of the difference in people. Some persons have the seemingly uncanny ability to tame all manner of snakes, while others get bitten by rosy boas!

Rainbow Boa (*Epicrates cenchria*)

This is a sluggish small boa, about six feet in maximum length, ranging from Central America to

Argentina. It has heat sensors like the Cuban boa and sometimes climbs trees after bats, but also feeds on small rodents and birds. It is gentle in captivity (except for the Argentinian variety).

Anaconda (*Eunectes murinus*)

This is the largest of the boas. It spends a good part of its time in water where it waits in ambush for animals to come to drink; it eats a wide variety of birds and mammals. Usually it is more aggressive than the boa constrictors, but I have nevertheless seen 15-foot specimens so tame that children could play with them. (However, this should always be done under supervision.) Anacondas are good feeders and can usually be trained to eat dead animals. This is especially handy, because the snake keeper can, if he wishes, freeze up a supply of rodents and thoroughly thaw them out when the anaconda is ready to eat (about once every two weeks to a month for very large specimens and a little bit more frequently for small ones).

Reticulated Python (*Python reticulatus*)

Although the longest snake known (but not the heaviest), the reticulated python eats mainly small mammals. This species appears often in shops. It can usually be tamed, but some specimens are pretty ornery

Different snake species have different habits, and these habits vary from individual to individual. Observe your snake in order to learn its particular likes and dislikes.

Above: *The Indian python,* Python molurus molurus. *This close relative of the Burmese python is smaller, has a better personality, and hails from India and Pakistan.* **Opposite, top:** *The reticulated python,* Python reticulatus, *is perhaps the longest snake in the world.* **Opposite, bottom:** *The blood python,* Python curtus, *is a small species from Malaysia, Borneo, and Indonesia.*

critters. If handled, they hiss and strike viciously. The longest recorded length is 32 feet. The female lays between ten and 80 eggs and coils her body around them until they hatch. The young hatch after about ten weeks and are about two feet long. Like the boas, this python will feed on pinkies when small, graduating to baby chicks, then small rats, and finally to full-grown rats.

Burmese Python (*Python molurus bivittatus*)

This python has been regularly available in pet shops. Unfortunately, its disposition is not as good as the very similar Indian python (*Python molurus molurus*), whose export has been restricted. Of course, the reader should be aware that he is taking a gamble any time he buys a python in the sense that it may or may not become tame. Still, even if it doesn't, that doesn't mean that it won't be interesting to keep. A snake does not have to be handled constantly in order to be a source of enjoyment. Individuals with particularly evil dispositions will hiss and threaten to strike at everyone that approaches their cage. Some snake keepers would be inclined to get rid of such a specimen. Others would appreciate the animal for its unbroken spirit. After all, it is a snake such as this that most resembles its brethren in the wild. Just because you can appreciate

such a specimen, though, doesn't mean that others will, and seeing the antics of such an animal may scare "ordinary" people to death and add to their prejudice against snakes. So, be careful how you introduce such a snake to the "noncombatants"! Well, anyway, let's hope you get a tame one, as this is a beautiful species and an efficient constrictor. In the wild it has been known to take surprisingly large prey. Reproduction is the same in this species as with other pythons. It reaches a length of about 18 feet.

Ball Python (*Python regius*)

This snake generally has a good disposition. It derives its name from its habit of coiling into a "ball" when frightened, with its head hidden in the middle. It can even be rolled across the floor in this mode and not change from the ball position. With handling, the snake will no longer retain that form when picked up (after it gets used to it), but it will often sleep in the position that gave it its name. In addition to the good disposition, the ball python is small, especially for a python, averaging about three feet in length.

Green Tree Python (*Chondropython viridis*)

This species is rare and extremely expensive. It is certainly not for the novice snake keeper; however, I am listing it as a point of interest. Its resemblance to the

A variety of Lampropeltis triangulum, *this snake is sometimes called the Honduran milk snake.*

emerald tree boa is remarkable in both appearance and habit. It is an excellent example of convergent evolution, in which two lines from different origins reach a very similar end point.

Above: Lampropeltis triangulum annulatum, *a milk snake from Mexico.* **Below:** Lampropeltis getulus californiae, *the ringed phase of the California mountain kingsnake.*

Above: The San Diego mountain kingsnake, Lampropeltis zonata pulchra, *from southern California.* **Below:** Lampropeltis pyromelana pyromelana, *the Arizona mountain kingsnake from Arizona and Mexico.*

FAMILY COLUBRIDAE

The number of species in this family outnumbers all the other snakes combined, so it is no surprise that the bulk of our species will come from this group. Although some of the members of this diverse family do contain venom, only a handful are of any danger whatsoever to man. In any case, we will list only the completely non-venomous species.

Garter Snakes (*Thamnophis*)

Members of this genus are the most numerous and far-reaching of the American snakes. Because of their ready availability, they are excellent snakes for the beginner. A garter snake is an alert little snake and is easy to keep since it eats goldfish. Since it can take only small food, it feeds more frequently than other snakes. (Most snakes can be fed about every ten days or two weeks.) For that reason, its cage may have to be cleaned more often. Its water bowl should be changed regularly, as fecal matter will occasionally be deposited there. Although the bite can scarcely be felt, freshly caught garter snakes are wild and will strike savagely. A good way to tame them (as with many other snakes, too) is to pick them up on cool mornings. They will be slightly sluggish then and will be seeking warmth. Thus, your body will be an attraction to them. With all snakes, it is best to lift them from underneath, giving them as much support as possible; try to avoid giving them the impression of being grasped or seized as though they were prey. There are many species of garter snakes, some more colorful than others, but most inhabit areas near water and prey on fishes, tadpoles, and frogs. They can reach a length of three and a half feet.

Common Garter Snake (*Thamnophis sirtalis*): There are several subspecies of this snake as, like many other snakes, it tends to vary somewhat according to distribution. The California subspecies has dull red side bands, some eastern subspecies have red spots, and some northern California specimens have blue stripes on the sides. All these have subspecies names (e.g., *Thamnophis sirtalis pickeringi* for the red-spotted variety). Young are born alive in all the garter snakes.

Western Garter Snake (*Thamnophis couchi*): This species ranges from Oregon to Baja California, from the coast to Nevada. Its color is highly variable, and it may or may not have stripes. It lives around ponds, lakes, brackish coastal waters, and even clear rivers high in the mountains. It feeds on tadpoles and fishes.

Checkered Garter Snake (*Thamnophis marcianus*): This is one of the most attractive garter snakes and is one of my favorites.

An interesting variety of the genus Lampropeltis. *Note the slight marks which are reminiscent of the fully banded kingsnake.*

It attains a size of about 42 inches and is rather heavy-bodied when compared with most other snakes of its genus. It is found in the southern part of California, Arizona, New Mexico, and nearly all of Texas and Oklahoma. Six to 18 young are born from June to August. It feeds on frogs, tadpoles, fishes, and crayfish.

Black-necked Garter Snake (*Thamnophis cyrtopsis*): This attractive little serpent is olive-gray with two large blotches on its neck separated by a black stripe. It ranges through Arizona, Utah, Colorado (southern portions), New Mexico, and parts of Texas. About seven to 25 young are born in the summer months.

Above: Thamnophis proximus, *a type of garter snake that is called a ribbon snake. It is more slender than most other garter snakes and is semiaquatic in some parts of its natural habitat.* **Below:** *A beautifully colored specimen of the eastern chain kingsnake,* Lampropeltis getulus getulus.

Above: The red-spotted garter snake, Thamnophis sirtalis concinnus, *ranges in a small area of Oregon and Washington.* **Below:** *A young eastern corn snake,* Elaphe guttata guttata. *In some forms of this snake, the reddish blotches are obscured by a bright pink to orange background color.*

RECOMMENDED SPECIES

Kingsnakes (*Lampropeltis*)

The kingsnakes are among the most impressive of snakes. They have everything going for them. They are as handsome as any snake, and some species are among the most beautiful of all snakes. They are generally hardy in captivity, some specimens having lived over 24 years. Ounce per ounce, they surely must be the most efficient constrictors. Unlike some other constrictors, they always seem to know exactly what they are doing. The fatal flaw, of course, is their diet. Oh, well, they will usually survive on a diet of mice and small rats. And if they do go off their feed, they are worth the time involved in gathering a few lizards or—perish the thought!—even snakes for food.

Common Kingsnake (*Lampropeltis getulus*): In California, this species is black with white to yellow rings, or it may be black with white (or yellow) longitudinal stripes. Other variations in the eastern and central U.S. are black with white chain markings, completely black with no other color, or black speckled with yellow. Females collected in the summer may be loaded with eggs. If a female you have purchased does lay eggs, they can be hatched by placing them in a gallon jug. Get sheets of paper toweling, wet them and wring them out, and place one layer underneath the eggs and one over them. Of course, the species can also be bred in captivity. In fact, Pat Cooney bred two color varieties together (ringed x lined) and got babies that were representative of each parent (some lined and some ringed) and some that combined the patterns. However, unless you are willing to go out collecting small lizards (which hatch about the same time as the kingsnakes), you had better forego breeding attempts. The eggs hatch in about three months.

California Mountain Kingsnake (*Lampropeltis zonata*): One of the prettiest snakes, it is also one that can be confused with venomous coral snakes (which, to be honest, are very unlikely to bite a human). In North America, coral snakes have the red ringed with yellow, whereas the kingsnakes have the yellow ringed with black. This pattern can be confusing to remember, so a silly little ditty can be of help here: "Red touching yellow can kill a fellow, Red touching black, poisons lack."

Unfortunately, this pretty species (sometimes called the coral king) is difficult to induce to eat mice. In the wild it eats lizards, snakes, and occasionally birds. Consequently, some will eat baby chicks in captivity.

Milk Snake (*Lampropeltis triangulum*): Another pretty snake with red (or orange), black, and yellow (or white) rings or blotches, this species receives its name from the notion that the snake takes milk from cows—which

76

The emerald tree boa, Corallus caninus.

makes about as much sense as most notions about snakes! They probably got their reputation from frequenting barns while looking for mice. Just imagine the number of these beautiful and beneficial snakes that have been killed by farmers who thought they were robbing the cows of milk! Since it is pretty and will take rodents, it is an especially good candidate for the snake keeper. It gets to be about 28 inches long. Some tropical subspecies get much larger. This snake ranges over all the eastern and central United States, with subspecies extending into South America.

Gray-banded Kingsnake (*Lampropeltis alternata*): Yet

Rat snakes are found in North America, Europe, and Asia, and they all look very much alike. **Opposite, top:** *A European species of rat snake,* Elaphe longissima. **Opposite, bottom:** *A striped Eurasian species of rat snake,* Elaphe scalaris, *which is quite similar to* Elaphe obsoleta quadrivittata. **Above:** *A rare Mexican species of rat snake,* Elaphe rosaliae.

another pretty kingsnake, this species is found in Texas and south into Mexico. It has white-bordered gray bands, alternating with black-bordered red or orange rings or blotches. It lays five to ten eggs from late May to July that hatch in about three months. Although preferring lizards and snakes, it will also take rodents.

Rat Snakes (*Elaphe*)

The rat snakes have some attractive species, particularly the corn snake, but they are not as efficient constrictors as the kingsnakes (always keeping in mind that individual snakes vary). Most of them are nocturnal, but they may also be out in late evenings or early mornings. Most rat snakes will take dead mice or rats, so it is probably best to thump the rodent on the head before offering it.

Corn Snake (*Elaphe guttata*): Some of these snakes are downright striking—especially the varieties from Florida—but others are nondescript, without a lot of color or definition in the pattern. Some say the name came from farmers finding the snakes in their corn fields. Another more convincing theory is that they were named after the checkered contrasting patterns on Indian corn, which the more colorful forms certainly resemble. This snake is a good climber and would likely appreciate a "tree" in its cage. It lays eggs which hatch in

about 64 days. It reaches a length of 72 inches.

Gray Rat Snake (*Elaphe obsoleta*): This species is not nearly so colorful as the corn snake, although some races are more colorful than others, having a little yellow in the pattern. It is a long snake reaching a length of over 100 inches. It lays clutches of between five and 30 smooth-shelled oblong eggs. Hatching varies with locality and temperature but usually requires between two and three months. It is a more powerful and slightly more skillful constrictor than the corn snake. It ranges throughout the southeastern United States.

Eastern Hognose Snake (*Heterodon platyrhinos*)

This species has several qualities to recommend it. First, it is a good feeder and will eat fishes, although it prefers toads. It almost never bites and is famous for its defense mechanisms. When threatened, a specimen puts on a fierce threat display. He "hoods" his neck like a cobra, hisses loudly, and strikes viciously (with the mouth closed!). If this fails, he writhes as though in his death throes, then turns over on his back, convincingly feigning death, mouth open and tongue lolling out. If he is picked up, he will hang limply in the hand—the perfect actor to the end! The only flaw in his "act" is that if he is placed back down on his belly, he

Snakes come with many different colors, patterns, dispositions, and appetites. There is something of interest for almost anyone.

promptly flops over on his back again. After capture, he may play possum for a few days every time he sees you, but, alas, after a while he no longer performs. Perhaps holding an unfamiliar animal (like a dog) up to the cage might induce a performance, but keep in mind that he has to be scared to perform, so to many of us the performance is not worth the "price."

This species mates in the spring and fall and lays anywhere from four to 61 elongate eggs about an inch and a quarter long. It usually places the eggs in a shallow cavity in loose or sandy soil. They hatch in about two months, depending on conditions, mainly temperature. It reaches a maximum of about 42 inches in length.

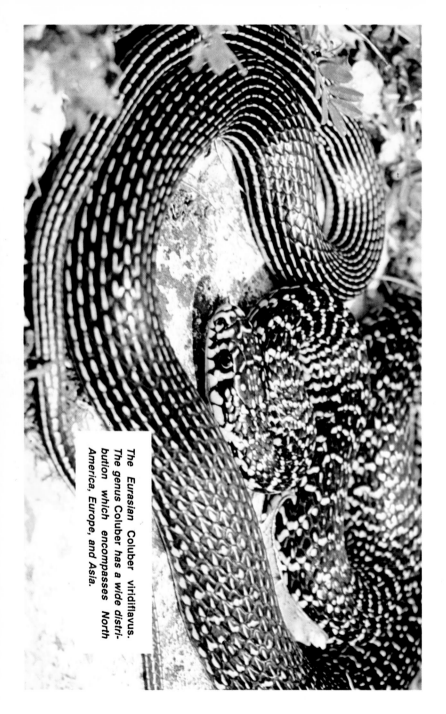

The Eurasian Coluber viridiflavus. The genus Coluber has a wide distribution which encompasses North America, Europe, and Asia.

Above: *A hatchling* Coluber constrictor, *the black racer. With growth, the blotches will fade until the snake is a uniform black to bluish black color.* **Below:** *The eastern hognose snake,* Heterodon platyrhinos. *This is a pale specimen in the cobra-like defensive pose.*

Western Hognose Snake (*Heterodon nasicus*)

This species has a more sharply upturned snout than the eastern hognose. It is also slightly less colorful, though neither species would compare with the kingsnakes. Although it will play possum, too, it is not quite as elaborate and convincing an actor as the eastern hognose. It breeds from March to May, and the eggs hatch out from June to late August. The young are about seven inches long, and adults can reach up to 36 inches in length.

Black Racer (*Coluber constrictor*)

In a field of prairie dogs, more years ago than I care to remember, a group of four young boys surprised a snake out in the open and chased after it, pelting it with rocks. The snake fled toward a rock pile but became trapped in an area where the boys could get up above it and rain rocks down upon it. They continued to stone it even after it was dead "just to be sure," then they went bravely down to inspect it. I was one of those little urchins, and I remember the sense of shame I felt even then upon inspecting the snake up close. For even though battered and bloody, it was a beautiful green serpent nearly seven feet long. In fact, it looked a little to me like the pythons that I had read about and seen in Tarzan movies. It was obviously not poisonous and had lived for some time to attain such a size— until four boys senselessly killed it. I am still not sure what the species was, for the memory plays tricks, but if I had to bet, I would guess that it was the green color phase of this species. If so, we killed a rodent and snake eater—not only a harmless snake, but a helpful and beneficial species.

This species has several color forms, but there are many reasons why it should not be kept. It can rarely be tamed, and it is restless in a small cage, frequently rubbing its nose raw. For the snake keeper who is willing to simply observe his charge and not handle it too much, however, this can be a fun-to-keep snake. I have been told of a man who, in addition to being a snake keeper, was a devotee of falconry. When it came time to feed the racer, a lizard was released in the house (obviously an understanding wife was involved!), then the racer was released to run him down, very much like a falcon after a rabbit!

Racers should be provided with an extra-large cage in which, in contrast to most snakes, they will be quite active, exploring it repeatedly. The cage should contain stones, branches, and other items for hiding and making the cage seem as natural as possible. Contrary to the scientific name, the species is not a constrictor. The breeding season varies according to the locality (it

A rainbow boa, Epicrates cenchria. *This species feeds on bats, small rodents, and birds.*

is found across the entire United States). Females lay five to 30 soft but rough-textured eggs which hatch in about nine weeks.

Coachwhip (*Masticophis flagellum*)

Like the previous species, this serpent is not highly recommended because it is restless in captivity, prefers a diet of lizards (but will eat rodents), and is too spunky to tame down

readily. Again, however, if the snake keeper is willing to provide a giant cage with branches and rock piles, he will have a fascinating show piece. The popular name for the snake obviously came from its resemblance to a braided coachwhip. From there it was a small jump to come up with stories about the snake chasing down humans and whipping them to death! (The public's imagination is

Above: *An indigo snake,* Drymarchon corais. *This snake makes an excellent pet but is not easy to find.* **Below:** *The European grass snake,* Natrix natrix, *makes a good pet. It is similar to the North American garter snakes.*

Above: A Caribbean boa, Epicrates inornatus. *Most Caribbean boas are rather aggressive and may not make good pets.* **Below:** *The pattern of the coachwhip,* Masticophis flagellum, *reminded people of a braided whip, hence its common name.*

a marvel, but its gullibility is downright disgraceful!) This species is not a constrictor, and it is as fast or faster than the racers.

Indigo Snake (*Drymarchon corais*)

The indigo has two main attributes going for it as a candidate for the snake keeper: it is pretty and eats almost anything. It is not a constrictor, but being a large snake (up to eight feet long), it can immobilize fairly large prey with its jaws. It is found in Georgia, Florida, Texas, and southward into Mexico. An egglayer, it deposits about five to 12 leathery eggs that hatch in about four months. The southeastern form is now endangered and rare.

Diamondback Water Snake (*Nerodia rhombifera*)

I debated with myself a little before including any of the water snakes (formerly *Natrix*), as they have an evil disposition and are difficult to tame. They are capable of inflicting a serious bite, so it may be time for the heavy gloves and jacket again. So why include the species? Well, first of all, they are easy keepers in that they will eat fishes, including thawed-out fillets cut to the right size for them. They are also hardy and are pretty. Occasionally they will become tame. In any case, I think more beginners become disenchanted with snake keeping

because they have a specimen that won't eat or becomes sick in other ways more than they do because they have an ornery critter that won't let them handle him. Rough stock is preferable to sick stock. It is depressing to have your animals do poorly, and, conversely, it is a source of genuine satisfaction to have them healthy and thriving. This species is heavy-bodied and gets to be about four or five feet long. It is greenish brown with large blotches on the back connected with alternating dark bars on the sides. It lives along the edge of bodies of water which it enters to forage for fishes and frogs. It is found in most of the south-central states and in Mexico. It mates in the spring. The 15 to 60 young are about nine inches long when born.

Northern Water Snake (*Nerodia sipedon*)

Another ornery-but-hardy water snake, this species is reddish gray or brownish black, depending on the locale. It mates in the spring, and 15 to 30 young are born in August to October. It is found in most aquatic situations, including salt marshes, and its range includes most of the eastern United States. It is active both day and night (depending on locale and time of year), and it feeds on frogs, fishes, salamanders, small turtles, crayfish, and even small rodents and shrews.

Eirenis collaris, *a small colubrid which eats small rodents, insects, and lizards.*

Gopher Snake (*Pituophis melanoleucus*)

It is fitting that we end with Arnold's species, for it is difficult to recommend any species more enthusiastically. Individuals can usually be tamed down, they eat well in captivity, and they are fairly efficient constrictors. This is a wide-ranging species covering most of the United States, barely intruding into Canada, and extending deep into Mexico. The color is going to vary somewhat, depending on where it is found. The eastern varieties (pine

Above and below: Bull snakes, or gopher snakes, the western subspecies of Pituophis melanoleucus, *are usually reddish brown, but there is quite a bit of variation among the many subspecies.*

Gopher snakes are hardy and make fine pets; their only drawback for beginners is their diet of small mammals.

snakes) are generally larger and often more difficult to tame. It usually mates in the spring and lays three to 24 eggs in burrows or in sandy soil in the shelter of rocks.

FURTHER COMMENTS

I have selected species on the basis already discussed, and I have left out species that are at all delicate. This includes most of the diminutive snakes that are recommended by other writers mainly because they are incapable of biting. Well, that is all to the good, but as I have already mentioned, there is nothing more likely to cause a sudden loss of interest in a hobby than failure. Besides, we want the snakes to do well, too, and to live long and happy lives. Speaking of that, the reader may be interested in how long his snakes will live. It is difficult to determine how long species live in the wild, so we have only their records in captivity to go by. The garter snakes live to ten years or slightly longer, kingsnakes and gopher snakes can easily surpass 20 years, and the giant boids will often make it past 30 years.

It is customary to designate snakes as constrictors or nonconstrictors, but there is no hard and fast line between the two groups, as occasionally a non-constrictor will utilize a coil to hold its prey down, while bona fide constrictors will often not bother to use coils on prey that they can handle easily. The advantage to being a constrictor is that the animal is able to handle much larger prey; in fact, many are capable of killing animals larger than themselves, and the kingsnakes will sometimes even engulf prey that weigh more than they do. Well, then, why aren't all non-venomous serpents constrictors? Apparently, in order to gain speed it is necessary to sacrifice the musculature necessary to be a good constrictor. Besides, certain types of prey just are not conducive to constriction (frogs and fishes, for example—not to mention certain insects).

It has been noted that almost all of our snakes put on a threatening display when frightened, distorting their heads or necks, hissing, and vibrating the tail. Some call this mimicry, as though all these snakes were pretending to be rattlesnakes. Another, and I think more logical, explanation is that this is just a pattern of threat display that is common to most snakes. It has evolved to a fine art in the case of the rattlesnakes with the development of the rattles.

There are many other questions and controversies that will be encountered by the snake keeper. Along with observing his charges and handling them and caring for them, it is part of the fun of being an ophiophile.

Index

BEGINNING WITH SNAKES
KW-127